Notes
—— about the ——
Constitution

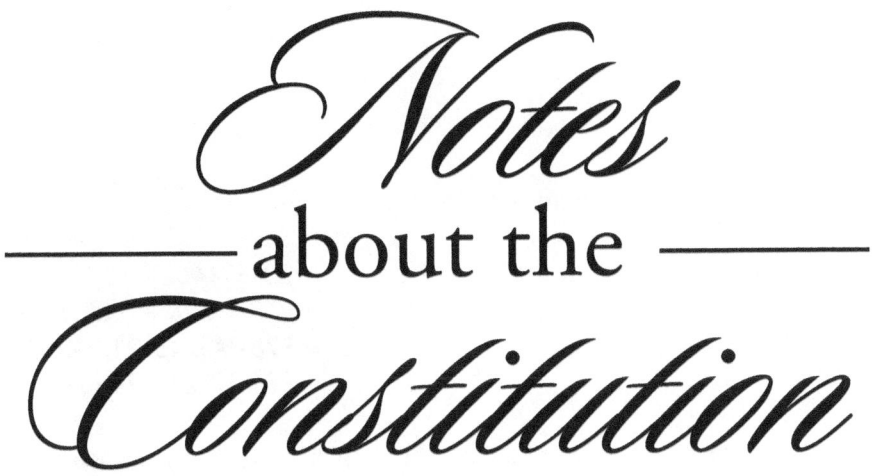

BAHADIR GEZER

e-mail: <u>bahadirgezer@hotmail.com</u>

Library of Congress Control Number:		2016914621
ISBN:	Hardcover	978-1-5245-9432-9
	Softcover	978-1-5245-9431-2
	eBook	978-1-5245-9433-6

Print information available on the last page.

Rev. date: 11/03/2016

To order additional copies of this book, contact:
Xlibris
800-056-3182
www.Xlibrispublishing.co.uk
Orders@Xlibrispublishing.co.uk
736058

CONTENTS

NOTES ABOUT THE CONSTITUTION

Time and Creation... These are the main focus of the Constitution I would say. Why?.. How?..

Let's go by order at the progress:

At the first paragraph of the Constitution we get the telling: "We the People of the United States... establish this Constitution for the United States of America.". This means it's USA's duty to apply the Constitution written by the People of the United States. Therefore USA also is meant to play a leading role at the establishment of the United States among the World with the support of the described (at the Constitution) States around the Globe with Time.

This I tell myself simply as this: why doesn't the first paragraph go like (sorry) this; "We the People of the United States... establish this Constitution for the United States."?.. no... because historically and World beneficially, a Constitution designed for a future and wide Time Unificationing State (the U.S.) to become fully be accepted by such a State such as USA is a strengthening sign of that Unification to become true in Time.

All this can also be explained with the opposite view to the subject. That would be the first paragraph of the Constitution to be taken as; "since the Constitution is established for USA, then we can threat the non-USA as different than the Constitution requires..." this "opinion" can't be, because the very same Constitution described USA (indirectly) as/within the U.S., which of course means that USA is meant to threat the States of the Globe as the Constitution requires due to the wide (broad) meaning of the United States... such as United States of the World, of the Solar, of the Milkway, of the Universe... The United States, alone is a very unification calling name for a form of an organization for the States of the World. All I'm saying is that as the "States" of the World, the "United" part should be handshaken over. Should be easy to understand as the States of the World that some State is just only by her Constitution telling clearly that these States should be United and be the United States. At this last sentence, the mentioned State is the USA.

But the very same (I'm sorry for being in need of the word: but) Constitution starts with the paragraph and at that paragraph the U.S. appear earlier than the USA. As I know from history, as the colonies were starting to fight with the B. Empire, to symbolize unification and democracy and independence they used the name "the United States". Then when the Time of declaration of the Constitution and the State and the rest has come (what's rest?.. I'll investigate... in west tee gate...) the newly formed organization's name has been the United States of America, adopting the Constitution written by the People of the United States. And as we will read more of the Constitution, we will understand that the 'phrase'; the United States, as a phrase at the Constitution represents the future more with her non-areal name. USA chosen by Time, Faith and History to help the setting of the United States among the World (as the Constitution says "time to time" over and over again, it could be among the Universe by Time as I said before)... To do this the USA needs to read the "time to time" message very well and needs to see what's written on the Constitution meant then and today is actually carrying, holding different meanings. This document carries different meanings for different Times of Time. This could easily be explained in one example: 400 years later from now, the People might use many words with different meanings than today, which could be a situation that can be today also. This situation might affect the Public understanding of the Constitution too. And yes, perhaps some new meanings might appear. And we shouldn't be worried about that because the writers of this document, very well observed and experienced the future and considered this as they were taking all this into recording.

As the Constitution gives this message about Unification and Time, the very crucial matters of belief(s) are simply, clearly put at front of the readers' eyes. By the way beliefs I said as plural with a little hesitation, because there's the message of the belief of creation (therefore God) at the Constitution, then belief of freedom of speech, then belief of every person to be equal and so on... But all these beliefs actually unite at the first mentioned belief of the previous sentence.

*With the name "the U.S." first appearing in the history, the ideal of uniting the States of existence has found a place on official document.

--- --- --- ---

What I clearly mean is that as the Founding Fathers of the State were taking all this into writing, when they said "the United States", they've mentioned an institution of the future which sets Peace and Unification within the environment. That's the Earth today, should be the Universe tomorrow.

While mentioning this, they named the new found State as the United States of America, and they clearly tied her with the United States, and they did this because they actually told us that the United States is an institution World widely international, and the United States of America is a State on an –mentioned on the name-area. The USA should be the leading State of the settlement of the U.S., but the USA alone shouldn't claim to be the U.S. .

The appearance of the U.S. as an international and wide unifying institution in Time clearly depends on how we read the Constitution which is written by the People of the U.S. for the USA and how we understand and apply it.

Personal Note:

Here, at this part of my life I got to admit that who would care about a World united?.. People have hard Time in having smiles, tears of smiles have not been dropping off our eyes for long long Time. The way we talk, act, eat, walk is messed up and even jam doesn't even sound. Yes, jam doesn't even sound these days. No one cares about the other one. People are stressed with the worries of life. A united World?.. would a united World make your Child the happiest inonaround Universe as any other Child?.. now that's why when I nonstoppingly am giving a speech about how the U.S. should be declared already, it obviously sounds weird. I'm saying that as We the People should understand from the name of the U.S. that the U.S. is an international name. Japan is a State, Turkey is a State, Mozambique is a State, France is a State, USA is a State... and it's USA's duty to set the U.S. among the World with the help and guidance of the secret and open messages of the Constitution of the USA written by the People of the U.S. (meaning: by the People of a United, Peaced Time). Now I'm sure that I don't need to give a history lesson here but it's clear that the Constitution shows this, shows all of this by the use of the phrase "time to time" over and over again. I'm in need of telling these to many and many and looking for support, but seriously... this have been within me for long Time and I'm still not done nothing about it. Sadness, hopelessness... Plus I tell myself; well the

Constitution is written already, these are gonna be done rightly today or tomorrow or whenever anyways. But signs, clear signs of lateness have shown up already even though we tried to avoid them for a long Time, and still, I still am not finding all the focus that I need to write findings of my honesty on the Constitution. What part actually means what to me, and what part means what to some as I observe.

Add to the personal note: Still I'll never loose the belief of a World which is unified by a Union of the States who are known can/will cause a betterization at every single Person's life on Earth. The outlook of the World will change, Peace will settle, Economy will boom, Natural Habitat will be conserved and secured better by the new settlement of the population of the Globe. So even when I'm at the maxi-edge level of the depression if I'm asked; "would a United World make a difference at your own life?" I would definetly say: yes. Yes with no hesitation. It will cause the starvings to come to an end, it will make the cities and towns become safer, it will cause peace among the Earth, it will make the technologic developments to become more wider spread with more availability, it will cause the health standards to rise Globally, as it will make a villager to be able to have constant water available at his/her house in Africa (if he/she desires) it will also cause a teacher or miner to pay the bills of the month in an easier way while producing more with the motivation caused by the right, good, justified environment by the Unity, and it will do more and more. That's why this Constitution of the United States of America is very crucial for me as it's giving direct information about the United States.

A brief West Coast look and explanation of what's told above:

-USA is a State who has adopted the Constitution written by the People of a State from future among Universe called the U.S. .

-USA is a State who has adopted the Constitution of a State from future called the U.S. . This "United States" at early Times stood before 'of America'. Same "United States" in Time will stand before "...of the World", "...of the Solar", "...of the Milkway", "...of the Universe".

(A Scenario!: "Sir... we just found out that in the history of the future, in order the United States of World, then the United States of Solar, then the United States of Milkway, then the United States of Universe will/has been established. It's our duty to find out which era the Constitution of the United States of America came from..." "what do you mean 'came from'?" "mind sir... human mind... and what the mind can do once you talk to Time." "what?" "I'm sure that you've read the book 'Alice's Adventures in Wonderland' sir. There the Hatter says to Alice: "I dare say you never even spoke to Time!" and Alice replies: "Perhaps not, but I know I have to beat time when I learn music." And the Hatter says: "He won't stand beating." Do you understand sir?.." "no I do not." "well if beating the Time means to travel through it, then it's prohibited because of the termination it might cause. But the Constitution shows that it happened. And Alice actually gives an idea about how it happened. Not by a machine, but by a State of Mind that's caused by the high sense of feelings with music, nature, creatures, Life all together, Time and of course the Trust in

God. Some can travel through Time at wherever they are by the State they get into. And Alice gives an idea about how it actually happens. But she has a wrong cause (aim), which is to beat the Time. But that's because of her innocence. She doesn't know much about Time. It's understood from the way she talks about it. The Hatter capitalizes, but Alice doesn't." "what are you on Earth talking about?" "We need to find out from which era of the future, from which form of the United States era, the Constitution of the United States of America came from.")

--- --- --- ---

After this explanation about the beginning of the Constitution, I jump to the Section 5 of the Article I; "Each House shall be the Judge of the Elections...". This is the very beginning of the section. I got to confess: I haven't read the Constitution with just one perspective. I naturally looked at it while feeling that every word could have bunch of meanings. At this section I took the word "house" as a regular house. A regular, random citizen house. This probably made it easier for me to take the Constitution as an issue of home.

At this section, I believe there's a very futuristic call for democracy. This section also is a proof that this Constitution can boost the productivity of ideas and materials at many different areas from arts to science. Why?.. How?.. So;

This section tells that every house should be taking active participation at the elective progress. That means this; you know that we have this tv channel on cable and satellite about the Senate and Congress right?.. It's a channel that broadcasts the progress about passing bills and stuff, and we got to admit that it's usually boring to watch what's going on that tv channel. It's boring because we do not take participation at what's going on while we're watching. And the Constitution tells us that we should.

What I mean here is that this section told me this: Put a camera into the screen of each television at each house. This camera will be used for a facial check for identification safety while taking direct participation on the bill passing or decision taking progress. The tv watcher will sit in his/her house at front of the tv while watching the Senate broadcast and will vote for a "nay" or a "yea" for the matter that's being argued by a remote control that puts in password and the option that's chosen and stuff. In detail this thing will work like this: The Senate let's say if has 50 Senators who vote for bills and take decisions for the People, then 20 chairs will be added to that Senate for the direct vote of the citizens. Citizens can, with an electronic device -which is safe about identification and more- participate on the matters that are being issued at the Senate or Congress and use direct vote just like a referendum (But while a referendum takes days to organize just like Elections, this system will work within minutes by the secure online system). USA can come up with the technological devices and Public network that supports this kind of a democratic system. This will give a new breath to democracy. People will feel the affect of democracy in a more obvious way. And this is so possible to set within a short period of Time. Of course a percentage of affectivity at the total rates of votes for the direct votes of the citizens should be set to not avoid the affectivity of the senators and the congressmen, congresswomen.

These I believe is the message of the very first sentence of the section. Addressing directly the houses of the citizens.

--- ---

I'll go on with the same section, which is the Section5 of the Article I..; "Each House shall keep a Journal of its Proceedings, and from time to time publish the same...". Now as told earlier, I take the word the "house" at this sentence as a regular house. Which means here the Constitution talks about my house, your house, our houses. And the Constitution's message is clear; writing down what's happening. Keeping record in a literal way. Now if every house in the State, within the borders of the State did what's told at this sentence, then the rapid rise at the ideas would cause fastening at the developmental progress for the humanity. This sentence personally affected me a lot because this is what I try to do. I see, feel the Habitat as my House and try to write down what I feel in/on/around here. I feel that it's my natural obligation and duty. And I feel and see that the Constitution of the USA also tells this.

--- --- --- ---

Next I'll talk about the Section 6 of the Article I. Some parts of this section I believe was written by the Natives by smoke to the air and the People who knew how to read the smoke writings put these onto paper. And this is how this section has developed.

This section carries a special place for me because of "...the Authority of the United States, which shall have been created..." part. "which shall have been created...". Now we should all know that creating is an action which can be done only and only by Creator; God. And the writers of the Constitution were naturally aware of that and that's why they've put this verb "create" into Constitution. By doing this, they have given motivation to those who have been believing into the ideals of the U.S. . Unification, peace, commonwealth, equality, natural rights of livings (inhabitants).

This matter also gives me the opportunity to declare that I'm against the use of the word 'create' in such sentences, such as; "it's a very creative idea.", "by doing this, we'll create many jobs.", "it's duty for us to create some new material that we can benefit from as humanity..."... no, no, no... Creating is an action which can never be done by the created. We can produce, make, invent, explore. But We can't create. This is one of the main things to know about being a created. So that means all these sentences at quotes in this paragraph are extremely wrong in use and even are innumerable.

On the Constitution however, the use of the word 'create' is a clear reminder of God.

(How many Constitutions do we know which secularly consider this matter in this kind of a proper, well and naive way?)

--- ---

Same section's (Section 6) last three lines makes me feel like I'm having a chat with a Native American who actually is telling me that whoever has an office under the U.S. should not have a certain house and realize that everywhere is his/her house; "...and no Person holding any Office under the United States, shall be a Member of either House during his Continuance in Office." This maybe a little hard to understand in the Times in which we make almost all our plans about having a nice house, car and being able to pay the monthly bills and stuff. But we got to look to the matter in a more Native way probably. Since the U.S. represents the institution which unites the States of the Habitat, then the officers of that institution should feel the whole of the Habitat as their house, and give up the comfort to live on a certain spot for the sake of the unification and peace.

And of course, as you would guess, in this section I again understood the "house" as a regular house. As a house.

--- --- --- ---

Section 8 of the Article I brings something completely new for the concept of the State. The section tells "The Congress shall have Power To lay and collect Taxes...". Now as the history of the civilization has shown to us, every State that has depended on a constant tax based system at some point has fallen. I'm not saying that tax is reason for a State to come to an end but the constant taxing certainly can be one of the reasons. And the Constitution has told this to us long ago.

What I mean is that at the first sentence of this section, the phrase "lay and collect" actually represents the opposite meanings. Lay here means leveling the taxes, which means a tax-free period for the State.

What I'm saying is that the Constitution clearly tells that one of the parties at the Elections can stand for a tax-free period. This would cause a boom in economy. Rapid rise at the investments and will also force the State to become more of a profit based institution.

At this day "laying" usually is being taken as "giving out" or "to distribute" at the meaning... But when I hear the word "lay", I think of laying down. I think of getting on ground level. I think of resting. And I sense that the Constitution here used this language for the tax-free period for the State message to be understood on the right Time of the history.

If/when I get the chance, I would like to answer questions about how a State economically can stand straight without tax.

--- --- --- ---

Another issue to settle the U.S. is the issue of the citizens of the USA to leave the USA to go to other States to work. This is a very important issue. For example Rome has failed because it did not carry some of its intellectual Roman population to the newly added lands of the State. Today USA's effect is World wide due to her citizens' perspective of life (optimist and welcoming to the new), to her economic and political standing, and to the developments in the areas of arts and science. Therefore USA needs to carry some of her population to these affected areas of the Globe in order to motivate the affected parts and defend the ideals of the U.S. in a natural way.

In a more clear way: Since the World is getting affected by the USA in some way or another it would be motivational for a Person to see an American in his/her daily life at/around his/her own habitat. This will make the Person realize that an American feels every part of the Habitat worth to live on, due to his/her cultural/natural tradition from the Constitution. Americans living abroad in this way will cause a positive movement at the motivation of the ideal of the United States. And the ideal of the United States should be to make the States that are known through the Habitat become united under the name of "the United States".

With this issue, it's proper to enter into the Section 9 of the Article I: "The Migration or Importation of such Persons as any of the States now existing shall think proper to admit, shall not be prohibited by the Congress prior to the Year one thousand eight hundred and eight, but a Tax or duty may be imposed on such Importation, not exceeding ten dollars for each Person."

At this section the word "State" represents not the States within the USA (since USA is a one State) but the States such as England, France, Turkey and USA. Why would the States within the USA charge anything from each other like a border or visa rule?.. This section abeles anyone around the Globe, who is a citizen of a State which has been declared before 1808 to freely migrate to the USA. With this the population of USA today would be around 700-500 million and that would cause a wider work and consuming force, larger productivity at the USA, and a more balanced population rate and economical settlement throughout the Globe. This isn't about the whole World rushing into USA if the section gets read carefully, because the section in detail tells that prior to the year 1808 the talked about States shall be already declared. That's why I said States like England, Japan, China, Turkey (A President of the USA, while giving a speech in Meclis talked about Turkey saying "Turkey" while talking about the Time of the Ottoman Empire era. That's a proof that as the Turkish society, the USA also accepts Turkey as the same State as Ottoman Empire. Well obviously Turkey did pay the economic obligations of the Ottoman era.), Germany, France and many other States that have been established and declared before 1808. And what about the People living in the other States?.. The Constitution at some other parts tells about what the inhabitants should do. So about what the People who live outside of those States may/can do, we got to read the parts that talk about the inhabitants at the Constitution. Now if we do that we will see that those People can first migrate to those States that are established before 1808 for a certain amount of Time and then think proper and pay maximum 10 Dollars and get a Duty and then can migrate to USA for instance. But is the World gonna be a better place just by USA allowing the migration policy that the Constitution requires?.. Well when the Constitution gets restarted to be applied fully (needed renaissance at the understanding of the Constitution of the USA) by USA as at this matter, the whole World won't be rushing to migrate into USA as some fears later on. Since this is told by the Constitution, applying it won't cause any trouble. In Time it shall be observed that the migration when applied as it's told, will be both ways with proper thinking, and will cause positive effect on both the USA and the World and therefore will serve the purpose of the U.S. .

By the way this phrase "proper thinking" at this section, is one of the motivating sayings that makes me come up with all this from my reading of the Constitution.

--- ---

1-why is migrating to USA such an issue?

2-should an American be afraid of migrators because migrators might be many?

1-because USA is the State that had adopted the Constitution written by the People of the U.S. . The U.S. always will represent the institution/ agreement of the United standing of the States of the known existence.

2-nope. Because 1808 rule, duty law... all this will add so much to both USA and USA's workforce. Today the American population should be around 600 million, 150 million living abroad, defending the ideals of the U.S. . The ideals of unification and peace. Of course I'm not telling People to do these all together just for unification and peace. This is to feed our stomachs properly. To be healthier and safer. Plus since there's the 1808 rule, the People from States that have been declared after 1808 can first migrate to States declared before 1808 other than USA, stay there for a period of Time and then think proper and take a Duty and migrate to the USA because this information is from the Constitution established for the United States of America. As USA applies this Constitution fully, We can expect from ourselves, faith, history and future a sentence that goes like this: We the People of the United States... establish this Constitution for the United States.

Within that United States, the States of the World including the USA can stand among peace and rise.

Or...

--- --- --- ---

Article II Section 1:

Or the President of the USA shall make a clear declaration and explanation after taking the oath: "I do solemnly swear (affirm) that I will faithfully execute the Office of the President of the United States, and will to the best of my Ability, preserve, protect, and defend the Constitution of the United States.".

This oath is a clear sign that the President understands and realizes this "time to time" issue. The President of the USA basically declares the United States and gets threated in that way as well. But adding after this oath, it's Time for the President to make a simple, logical, understandable explanation and clear international declaration of the United States with the support of the told States at the Constitution. First the Union can be managed between the States that have been established before 1808 due to their historical and cultural experience about civilization (therefore about the Habitat and the Life). Then by Time all the States of the existence (including the USA) can be the part of the organization that's called the United States.

--- --- --- ---

-Do you understand this?.. At 2012 the phrase "the United States and the World" in a sentence shouldn't be. If We read the Constitution with the understanding of Time and Trust, We can easily come to the conclusion that at 2012 the United States, according to the Constitution written by the People of the U.S., already should have represent the unity of the States of the World.

We are late.

We need to speed up.

--- --- --- ---

Article III Section 2 carries special meaning for me as well as many other parts. What's up about this section is that; this section shows how the Constitution uses the word "State".

The Constitution uses the same word for both the State within Federal Organization and the State as the Authority over the Country.

In a more clearer way of saying; this section proves that this Constitution describes Germany, Turkey, England, Japan, France, China, Brazil, Ivory Coast, S. Africa, Italy and so on as "State", which is a proof that the same Constitution describes the USA as a State too. After seeing this obvious connection, We the People should know what "the United States" is calling us to do. And We should also be aware how the United States of America takes part within all this. "The United States" as I said before is a call to work for the unification of the States who are known. And this section proves to me that the Constitution is also written to be understood in this way by Time.

--- --- --- ---

About the amendments, what I feel pretty much is the same as I felt at 2007.

--- --- --- ---

Criticism of the United States of America:

Since the criticism can be beneficial for who ever is being criticized, I'm gonna talk about something that bothers me a little about what's going on in the USA about a specific matter.

Taxation without representation... I know that every American would be very sensitive about this. Every citizen of a State -whose Constitution is tied to the United States concept/ideal- should be feeling sensitive about this matter. Well let me tell you what happened to me:

I went to college in USA as an international student. And I've (my scholarship) paid around 20 thousand bucks a year. The school was charging this amount because around 2-4 thousand of it was going to the taxes that the school had to give in. So the school is being taxed on the charge that it gets from me. That means that I'm indirectly being taxed. I could pay around 15 thousand Dollars if I wasn't indirectly being taxed. I didn't have the right to vote in the USA, and because of my "visa" status I wasn't allowed to work. So obviously direct or indirect, I shouldn't be taxed while my declared to be for a temporary period of Time stay in the USA, because that would be taxation without representation right?

Well when the charges that the international students pay to the education institutions start to get constant tax-free as it should, then the international student rate in the USA will rise also which will help cultural interaction and economic movement and will cause the American students to do the same (going abroad, looking for experience of cultural variety) and these will all help the purpose of the United States.

This indirect taxation issue got clearer at my mind after I've read the Section 2 of the Article I and saw "direct tax" term. If there's direct, then there's indirect also. This was my basic logic at this issue. And that reminded me this personal memory.

--- --- --- ---

(Written in Istanbul at 2012 after re-reading the Constitution and "the Constitutional Readance")

THE CONSTITUTIONAL READANCE

Before I started reading the Constitution I set up main questions that I am looking for answers... These questions are "What's the age of voting?", "What's the taxing age?", and "Why is there taxation?"

The first thing that I'm gonna say about the Constitution is that I feel like the text is coming from the future. Instead of seeing the Constitution as a historical document I rather seeing it coming from the future because of the very first sentence: "We the People of the United States...establish this Constitution for the United States of America." So it's like the people of the United States came from the future to the past to write this Constitution for the people of United States of America. That means one day

USA is going to become the US or part of the US. But for that USA needs to fulfill the Constitution which has been established by the people of the United States.

Then comes Article I. Section 1. "All legislative Powers...shall be vested in a Congress of the United States." As I read this I told myself that I need to double check how the Congress is following the Constitution.

Section 2 says "The House of Representatives shall be composed of Members chosen...of the several States..." then "...Representatives and direct Taxes shall be apportioned among the several States which maybe included within this Union..." So clearly some states within the Union, got to stand differently than the other states. But today it's hard to say "several states" when talking about USA, because it might sound dividing or separative. Of course there are differences between the states but there isn't a difference as clear as it's mentioned at the Constitution. This section might seem like its days are way past or even over but because of the rising population density and environmental reasons the section could still be effective. And also a trip to the Senate of the USA can make one have an idea about who these "several States" are. What I mean is that these States are the States such as France, Turkey and so on. What I mean in a clearer sense is that these "States" that are mentioned are not the States within the Federal Organization, they are to mean the Authority over the country while internationally being recognized. This shows that I also see the "Union" as mentioned here as the standing of the US as a Global Unifying Institution rather than just restrengthining the importance of the unification of the USA alone.

Section 3 follows: "...The Senate shall have the sole Power to try all Impeachments...".

Section 5: "...Each House may determine the Rules of its Proceedings, punish its Members for disorderly Behavior, and, with the Concurrence of two thirds, expel a Member... Each House shall keep a Journal of its Proceedings, and from time to time publish thee same, excepting such Parts as may in their Judgment require Secrecy..." Obviously the House of

Representatives is being talked about here. But I see it as a regular house issue. These could be the rules of a regular citizen house.

Section 6: "The Senators and Representatives... except Treason, Felony and Breach of the Peace, be privileged from Arrest during their Attendance at the Session of their respective Houses, and in going to and returning from the same; and for any Speech or Debate in either House, they shall not be questioned in any other Place..." This section should include the president also. And the section is not being followed at all in all parts... This is what I believe. But the scary thing is that if we asked 100 random people, 95 of 'em would say the same thing. And I just can't believe that some are seeing this subject as a "So what?" matter.

Then comes the Section 7, which is a warning section. Section 7: "...Senate may propose or concur with Amendments as on other Bills..." The section says that the Senate might do it. Senate might pass amendments, but it doesn't say that the Senate should. The amendments which have been passed, many of them are messed up. Article V also talks about amendments: "The Congress...shall propose Amendments to this Constitution..." It's not like I'm against all amendments, but some of them are ridiculous. I will talk about one of them in a short while.

Taxless state. This is my dream: living in a country with no tax. The business would rise rapidly. Development would boom. But the Section 8: "The Congress shall have Power to lay and collect Taxes, Duties, Imposts and Excises to pay...general Welfare of the United States; but all Duties, Imposts and Excises shall be uniform throughout the United States..." You can laugh at me now, but as I read this and as a person who started to speak English at the age of 16, I thought lay and collect must mean the opposites. What's said is clear, but this is followed by Section 9, which uses even a clearer language: "...No Capitation, or other direct, Tax shall be laid..." Now this was what I was waiting for! What does "laid" mean? I've met an American girl at a café in Istanbul, she was just sitting there enjoying her Efes, and I asked her what "laid" meant, she said "give out, distribute". That makes me want to say "No capitation, or other direct, tax shall be given out" and "given out" does not stand for giving, it stands for "giving up". But I still want to say that "laid" means "leveled". Or laying could mean abandoning or to renounce. The clause says "No capitation". That's pretty clear for me. Clearly taxation is being told to be put out. This is what can make a state become strong. I mean I am trying to use a simple language. Taxation makes the state collect money in an easy way and makes it easier for corruption to rise. Historically all the states which has been based on constant taxation system, have fallen. Instead of taxing, the state should be more Adam Smith style capitalistic, and collect money after giving the service... For instance a device could be put into a car to show how many miles it has been driven for the last 3 months and the owner could be charged over that. Instead of house taxation, automobile taxation, systems like this could be used. Examples could be multiplied to make a state based on profit. But instead of that the Senate and the Congress passed an amendment which gave birth to a main reason for World War I. I'm talking about Amendment 16: "The Congress shall have power to lay and collect taxes on incomes, from whatever source derived..." What does "whatever source" mean?.. This amendment was ratified at February 3, 1913. At 1914 the greatest war that the world has have ever seen took place. Why?.. Because even though the Congress doesn't clearly say it; to get money, gun producement has been increased. Thousands of young men has been sent to other places to find some sources to derive from. At the Article V it's said "...that no Amendment which may be made prior to the year 1808 shall in any Manner affect the first and fourth Clauses in the 9th Section of the 1st Article..." So I don't understand how the fourth clause of the Section 9 has been worked on by the Amendment 16.

There's something about Section 9: "The Migration or Importation of such Persons as any of the States now existing shall think proper to admit, shall not be prohibited by the Congress prior to the year 1808, but a Tax or duty may be imposed on such Importation, not exceeding ten dollars for each Person." Now as I've read this I was thinking about migrating to the US. I thought about taking a duty and I said American Dream: Duty is to become President. But seriously at that paragraph of the Section 9 as it says "...any of the States now existing..." it doesn't only talk about the states within the Union. And the Congress as the institution which holds all the legislative powers of the United States of America, does not have the right to stop a person who wants to migrate. But this includes only the states which was existing in the year of 1808. Still when I go to the embassy I don't see anyone very welcoming.

Article II Section 1 also talks about the President; "...Before he enter on the Execution of his Office he shall take the following Oath or Affirmation: "I do solemnly swear (or affirm) that I will faithfully execute the Office of President of the United States, and will to the best of my Ability, preserve, protect and defend the Constitution of the United States." As said one of the main obligations of the President is to defend the Constitution, therefore he is got to do something about the 1st and 4th clauses of the Section 9. Article I.

Article III. Section 1: "The judicial Power of the United States, shall be vested in one Supreme Court..." After reading this I thought about going to the Supreme Court about the 1st and 4th clauses of the Section 9. Article I, but the Amendment 11 says "The Judicial power of the United States shall not be construed to extend to any suit in law or equity, commenced or prosecuted against one of the United States by Citizens of another State, or by Citizens or Subjects of any Foreign State." So what can I do when I feel like the Constitution is being harmed? All I can do is to write and talk about it anytime when I get the chance.

The Article IV. Section 4 says "The United States shall guarantee to every State in this Union a Republican Form of Government..." Republic is the regime of the ideology called democracy.

The Article V. "The Congress...shall propose Amendments to this Constitution" Is there gonna be a time saying enough to it? "... that no Amendment which may be prior to the year 1808 shall in any Manner affect the 1st and 4th

Clauses in the Section 9 of the Article I..." So why were they changed?

Then start the Amendments... Amendment 1: "Congress shall make no law respecting an establishment of religion, or prohibiting the free exercise thereof; or abridging the freedom of speech, or of the press, or the right of the people peaceably to assemble, and to petition the Government for a redress of grievances." That's what should make it easier for you/me to sell whatever (including ideas or whatever books, CDs etc...) in the US market, and it's nice to see secularism being protected. Also when I saw the Constitution pointing out on the freedom of speech like that I thought about sending this understanding of a reading to the White House, Foreign Secretary and to the US consulate in Istanbul. But all the people I talked with about this issue told me that this was not a good idea.

The Amendment 4: "The right of the people to be secure in their persons, houses, papers, and effects, against unreasonable searches and seizures, shall not be violated /..." awesome! "...

and no Warrants shall issue, but upon probable cause/..." what? "... supported by Oath or affirmation, and particularly describing the place to be searched, and the persons or things to be seized." What?

The Amendment 5: "No person shall be held to answer for a capital..." brilliant but the amendment follows: "...unless..." why is there always a way of skipping the main point of the amendment?

Then we jump to Amendment 7: "In Suits at common law, where the value in controversy shall exceed twenty dollars, the right of trial by jury shall be preserved, and no fact tried by a jury shall be otherwise re-examined in any Court of the United States, than according to the rules of the common law." Would be nice...Would make it a lot easier for one to sue someone who is bothering him or herself. But is the value of controversy still gonna be 20$? And the Amendment 11 makes my dreams of suing people come to an end: "The Judicial power of the United States shall not be construed to extend to any suit in law or equity, commenced or prosecuted against one of the United States by Citizens of another State, or by Citizens or Subjects of any Foreign State." Well it's okay... I don't have trouble with no one in the US., all I want is to prosecute about the 1st clause of the Section 9, Article I.

Then the Amendment 9 leaves a nice implementation and the Amendment 10 tubs in: "The powers not delegated to the United States by the Constitution, nor prohibited by it to the States, are reserved to the States respectively, or to the people." Why would the powers not delegated to the US. by Constitution be tried to be taken into possession? The Amendment 13 makes a completely righteous point.

Then comes the Amendment 15 with its full logiced, easy to be understood, well made points: Section 1: "The right of citizens of the United States to vote shall not be denied or abridged by the United States or by any State on account of race, color, or previous condition of servitude." Section 2: "The Congress shall have power to enforce this article by appropriate legislation." The need of such amendment is a shame.

The Amendment 16 follows... I already did mention this amendment talking about "...from whatever source derived..."

The Amendment 17 is a little strange just like I am... the 1st clause of Amendment 17: "The Senate of the United States shall be composed of two Senators from each State, elected by the people thereof, for six years; and each Senator shall have one vote. The electors in each State shall have the qualifications requisite for electors of the most numerous branch of the State legislatures..." Why? Are the elections once in four years? Why are the elected by a general election staying less in office than the senators? Elected by some is staying longer in office than elected by all. When was this approved?.. Wait a minute... Ratified in April 8,1913. Then the 2nd clause of the amendment follows: "When vacancies happen in the representation of any State in the Senate, the executive authority of such State shall issue writs of election to fill such vacancies..." Still not talking about some amount of office time. The article continues: "...Provided, that the legislature of any State may empower the executive thereof to make temporary appointments until the people fill the vacancies by election as the legislature may direct..." What is a temporary appointment? No seriously... What is a temporary appointment?

Amendment 18 Section 1 is just dumb... there is no need to comment on it. Section 3 says: "This article shall be inoperative unless it shall have been ratified as an amendment to the Constitution by the legislatures of the several States..." What is the need to say this? I mean this is such a thing that wouldn't be needed to be said. How can an article be valid without being placed in the Constitution?

Then comes the Amendment 20 with its all logical Section 1,2 and 3. Then Section 5 passes by mentioning my birthday "...15th day of October..." Later comes the Section 6 like the Section 3 of the Amendment 18: "This article shall be inoperative unless it shall have been ratified as an amendment to the Constitution..." And I'm still asking what the need of saying this is. And an answer is popping up in my head: there is a risk of a document becoming a law without it entering into Constitution. But then this is what an amendment should come out about. Anyways...

The Amendment 22. Section 1. "... But this Article shall not apply to any person holding the office of President when this Article was proposed by the Congress, and shall not prevent any person who may be holding the office of President, or acting as President, during the term within which this Article becomes operative from holding the office of President or acting as President during the remainder of such term." Only one question: why? Why are they ratifying an amendment that they don't want to be affected by?

Then the Amendment 24. Section 1: "The right of citizens of the United States to vote in any primary or other election for President or Vice President/..." I think that the article keeps talking about the citizens... Basically the article is saying "The right of citizens of the United States to vote in any primary or other election; for President or Vice President, for electors, for Senator, for

Representatives" So basically these are what the citizens should vote for: President and Vice President, Elector, Senator, Representative... Of course this is how I understand it. I don't know how but some might understand something different from the rest of the section: "/...for electors for President or Vice President, or for Senator or Representative in Congress, shall not be denied or abridged by the United States or any State by reason of failure to pay any poll tax or other tax."

I started with three questions at the beginning... The answer of one of them was found on an amendment... The Amendment 26 Section 1: "The right of citizens of the United States, who are eighteen years of age or older, to vote shall not be denied or abridged by the United States or by any State on account of age." My question was the age of voting... I am actually shocked about not seeing that at the actual Constitution...

The weird thing of all is that for all those years while I was in the USA, I didn't care about talking about Constitution at all... At high school none of us read the Constitution... Well maybe some of us did... Not that I know...All I did was to read books, get high and play Playstation...In college it was pretty much the same...

The thing is: Why do I freaking talk about the Constitution? Why did I even read it?.. I'm not going to say that I don't read... I do read... I did and do read a lot... But never thought about reading the Constitution...I don't remember asking a friend of mine in the USA "Hey!..Did you read the amendment 16 on the Constitution?" if anyone said anything like that we would be like: "What on Earth are you talking about?" Not to go too far but seriously... I never thought about reading the Constitution...So what's the big deal?.. The big deal for me is that I've enjoyed reading the Constitution... It also made me think... So what?

There is a bigger deal for me even... is the 1st clause of Section 9 Article 1... That paragraph made me think with migrating in my mind. Made me start thinking properly. And all of this is what that section says basically "The Migration...of such Persons as any of the States now existing (Doesn't say State within Union.) shall think proper to admit…" and that's exactly what I'm doing…The article continues: "… shall not be prohibited by the Congress…" That means anyone from an existing State can go to the USA, anytime… That's how I see it… And that's why I talk about it. Because there isn't anyone to talk about it, I just write and also search for some answers. Pfffffff I want to learn for sure to see if the United States law legislation sees the 1st clause of Section 9 Article 1 the way I see.

My question about the "taxing age" has been left unanswered. Maybe an age for taxing should be set…But I'm against taxation after all.

Briefly this is all that I get from reading the Constitution for the first time. I hope that it makes sense to everyone the way it made sense to me.

(Written in Istanbul at 2007 after reading the Constitution)

RANDOM NOTES

A synopsis:

MOHAMMAD AGAIN

A piece of the hair of Prophet Mohammad is kept and shown to public at the Topkapı Palace Museum in Istanbul. This is real.

What's gonna happen is that that piece of hair gets stolen by some people. And after they steal it they find a way to brake the DNA code of Mohammad from that hair piece. After they brake the code they find a way to clone Mohammad and many incidents happen after that.

Eulogy to the USA: Many years ago, when I was before twenty-one ages of old and was living in USA on my own... the social security office issued me with a security, because -I believe- I had no relatives or nothing like that within USA. This sounded not just nice but also fair to me. My S.S. is issued by the state Connecticut (Connect I Cut... ok, was a bad joke... but connect I cut is awesome for a Connecticuter because from one point that's getting to Connect I Cuter... I cuter I cuter... yeah I am simply getting more cute than you even...)

From a dialogue:

-Some might say that "for a world which is united, there is a pure action of the United Nations (the UN.) instead of the name; The United States."

What I can say about this is that; the every nation on the earth do not have a state. And the nations can't sign papers or nothing. But the states can do that for the name of the nations... A state also means a disciplined nation.

-The copyrights of the examination papers of students at the colleges/universities will/should be owned by the students. In this way we can read about Hussein Barack Obama -if he desired- when he was young for instance.

-Psychiatry and Psychology... Two words that does mean nothing to me. I mean literally; psychiatry means the "science of soul" and psychology means "logic of soul". When someone says "I am a psychiatrist", that person is simply saying "I am a soul scientist."! Where did you see the soul? How did you come up to the conclusion that the souls need treatments? If today you are "curing" the souls, who can stop you judging of those souls tomorrow? Who is the Judge, have you forgotten?

Since we treat 'the soul scientists' as doctors, we are living in a World like this; if I go out and start to make up with the tree right next to the me... French kiss and stuff with it!.. an ambulance would come right away and they would take me into a facility naturally... but in some parts of the World when two men or two women make out on the street, this illness is being seen as a choice... Is it the choice of a 4 year old nephew to see two men French kissing each other like it's a normal thing?

We are asking for a cure of an illness... Not an illness to become as a sign of good/normal health.

-Washington DisCipline

The languages all around the world are constantly improving and changing... now when I look at the word: American, I read the word as Amer I can... here I try to look at the words such as saf<u>er</u>, fast<u>er</u>, bigg<u>er</u>, bett<u>er</u>... er, er, er... this always meant more... therefore when someone says "I am<u>er</u>" he or she mentiones that he/she is not just saying "I am" but "I amer"... it's like saying; "I am not just I am, I actually amer"... When I look at the word American... Amer I can

The conditions of the languages... If/when looked to the original text of the Beowulf or the Shakespearian original texts, we can clearly see the former Englishs are different than today's... Looking at the picture with this perspective the word that the British royalty uses "sir" can actually mean: "simply I are"... This is pretty much the same logic that I've used looking at the word: American... One person is pluralizing himself.

-There is something called the language barrier. Just like the sound barrier it is material and a fact. Here is what language barrier is: The word "ass" in English -I mean the sound of the word- might mean "holly" in another language in let's say at a South American tribe. Or a sound of a curse might have total different meaning in another language. This is what the language barrier is. We simply got to work for the good words in our languages to not mean something bad in other languages.

-**Con. money**. Contemporary money. It has nothing to do with the concept of "temporary ". It's simply the money that catches the momently price of the value of the money. This comes from the logic that the 10$ bill in your pocket might actually be standing for 12$ right at that moment. I mean the 10 bucks at your pocket might be able to buy a service or products worth for 12 bucks at a moment. Con.money can be the electronical money that catches the every second value of the money. The every citizen should be served with the fairest possible economic system.

For beginners the credit cards can apply this system.

-Check this e-mail out!:

"> Date: Wed, 8 Apr 2015 09:07:07 -0400
> Subject: RE: www.whitehousegiftshop.com Order Confirmation
> From: whitehouse@whitehousegiftshop.com
> To: bahadirgezer@hotmail.com
>
> Hello Bahadir,
>
> I think there may have been a miscommunication issue somewhere along the line. When our shipping staff discovered this order we had to cancel it. I am sorry to say we have been experiencing issues with Turkey Customs where our items have not been delivered to them or rejected back to us but lost somewhere in the void. You should have received an email on the order cancellation.

Order notes from invoice: Special Note: Shipping to Turkey is not available at this time.

>

> I do apologize for any inconvenience this may have cause but we are unable to ship to Turkey. Your charge was voided so your card was not charged. I do apologize again.

>

> Thank you for your understanding and patience.

>

> Best Regards,

> Kat"

This is what i've received. I can buy on amazon.com, or on e-bay.com but not on whgiftshop.com?!!!!!!!!!

I'm victimized, the White House is victimized here.

Wake up not WH, just stop sleeping.

-the 4th w suggestion: we know that today in the world almost 95 percent of the web sites are starting with www first. We are taught that these 3 w letters stand for "world wide web ". That may be true but another meaning of it simply is "when where what". By the nature of internet and the ip numbers of computers and stuff, it's easy to see when a computer has been used, where it was used, and what was the content / aim of the user. But we do not know for sure who actually uses the computer. All I suggest is to put the 4th w to its' place. Fingerprint reading, face and breath recognizing computers...

-Let's say that at the beginning of the year 2 Turkish Liras was 1 American Dollar. Now it's almost 3 Turkish Liras equals to 1 American Dollar. So does it mean that American Dollar got stronger or more expensive? Does it mean that Turkish Lira got cheaper or weaker? Cheap and weak is not always mean the same, nor expensive and strong.

-capital = energy + source + tools + will of producing (the will of fullfilling one of the reasons of humans to be)

energy, source, tools, will of producing = human

Provider?

-We do hear and see a lot about the Air Force One... why do we not about when it comes to Sea Force One and the Land Force One?

-3D printing technology! Awesome! The doctors are printing organs and stuff. Amazing, cheeks numbing developments. Can we 3D print an Earth?

-freedom is not free. Therefore we shall let / set the freedom free.

Even the freedom isn't free... how can a human being, how can the World be free if we don't let/set the freedom free?

Freedom is not free... yes this doesn't only mean that there is a price for freedom.

Reader's Notes

Reader's Notes

Reader's Notes

www.ingramcontent.com/pod-product-compliance
Lightning Source LLC
Chambersburg PA
CBHW030529290526
45786CB00004B/1659